HAMPSHIRE

THE COUNTY IN COLOUR

IAN PARKER & BARRY SHURLOCK

COUNTRYSIDE BOOKS
NEWBURY, BERKSHIRE

COUNTRYSIDE BOOKS
3 Catherine Road
Newbury, Berkshire

To view our complete range of books,
please visit us at
www.countrysidebooks.co.uk

ISBN 1 85306 881 0

Photo on page 41 courtesy
of John Holder

Map on page 4 by Trevor Yorke

Designed by Peter Davies, Nautilus Design

Produced through MRM Associates Ltd., Reading
Typeset by Techniset Typesetters, Newton-le-Willows
Printed in Italy

CONTENTS

HOSPITAL OF
ST CROSS,
WINCHESTER.

KING ALFRED STATUE,
WINCHESTER.

Highclere
Silchester
Stratford
Saye Park
The Vyne
Beacon
Hill
BASINGSTOKE
Odiham
ALDERSHOT
BASINGSTOKE CANAL
Overton
ANDOVER
Alton
Micheldever
Chawton
Danebury
Hill
Longstock
Selborne
Stockbridge
New
Alresford
R. ITCHEN
WINCHESTER
Mottisfont
Shawford
Old Winchester
Hill
East Meon
BUCKLER'S
HARD
ROMSEY
Meonstoke
Butser
Hill
Rockbourne
EASTLEIGH
BARGATE,
SOUTHAMPTON.
Breamore
R. TEST
SOUTHAMPTON
Fordingbridge
Rufus Stone
Netley
Portchester
R. MEON
Minstead
Bursledon
Emsworth
Lyndhurst
Hamble
Warsash
Southsea
Beaulieu
NEW FOREST
HAYLING
ISLAND
Burley
Beaulieu
Bucklers
Hard
GOSPORT
N
PORTSMOUTH
Lymington
THE SOLENT
BEAULIEU
ISLE
OF WIGHT

HAMPSHIRE

HMS VICTORY, PORTSMOUTH.

INTRODUCTION

Visiting Brittany a few years ago and listening carefully to a furniture restorer speaking French, I thought I detected an English accent. 'You're from the UK aren't you,' I said. 'No, mate, I'm from Yorkshire,' came the reply. The man was rightly proud of his roots in a county that has played more than its fair share in national history: Hampshire is in the same league, another 'super-county'.

The photographs taken specially for this book by Ian Parker start in the south-west of the county, depicting the ports of the western Solent and the New Forest. They then run up the river Test to the high lands of North Hampshire, before returning south via the county capital, Winchester, to the Sussex borders, Portsmouth, Spithead and the eastern Solent.

Hampshire can be divided into at least three major areas, each with its own character and history. Coastal Hampshire is concerned with defence, commerce and sailing. Here it has often been at the centre of national events, from the departure of Henry V and his army from Southampton for Agincourt to the massing of troops for D-Day. The Navy's 'arms race' has driven the local economy and spilled over into its industry. Since the early 1800s, and especially since the last war, the business of sailing for pleasure has moved front stage. Southern Hampshire – and perhaps even more so Farnborough, in the north – had a central role in the development of aviation. Elsewhere in northern Hampshire, notably in Basingstoke and Andover, the influence of London has been the driving force for change and development, whilst in the centre of the sandwich stands Winchester, once the capital of 'Saxon England' and now a pleasant county town surrounded by rolling hills and charming villages.

There are an overwhelming number of places to visit in the county, including many that have a tale to tell – often of national importance – as well as others where the main emphasis is on fun. There are countless ways of life on the Hampshire coast, in the busy cities of Southampton and Portsmouth, and the inlets and harbours of the Solent; in the New Forest, rich in natural history and archaeology; along the celebrated Test and Itchen; in Winchester and its surroundings; in the towns and on the downs of northern Hampshire. This book offers a taste of the riches that are to be found in a 'super county' that has rarely needed to extol its attractions.

Barry Shurlock
July 2004

THE NEW FOREST

The New Forest, recently designated a National Park, is a vast area of heathland, bog and woodland in the south-west corner of Hampshire, with Lyndhurst as its capital. Until modern times it was virtually deserted, but now attracts large numbers of visitors. It is a paradise for walkers, naturalists, picnickers, orienteerers, archaeologists and anyone who likes to 'get lost' easily and explore a place that reeks of days gone by. The contrast between the urban jungle to the east of Southampton Water and the forest could scarcely be greater; it is the main reason why it is such a popular attraction, especially being so close to the intense development that is Southern England and yet so far from that way of life. Protecting it is a huge challenge and a major preoccupation for the verderers, as the members of the governing body of the New Forest are called.

The few villages in the forest are without exception a delight. Places such as Fritham, Burley (*opposite*), Minstead and East Boldre are all memorable and have an alluring remoteness, except perhaps Burley at the height of the cream-teas-and-coach season.

Happily situated in the heart of this arcadian setting is Beaulieu, which takes all seasons in its stride and is a visitor attraction of international renown. One of the star exhibits is the National Motor Museum (*inset*), created by the present owner, the 3rd Baron Montagu of Beaulieu. He was one of the first owners of stately homes to realise that the only way to retain his great estate was to open it to the public.

It is ironic that the New Forest is such an attraction in our times, because historically the poverty of the soil made it relatively under-populated. Whilst farmers in the corn belts of Hampshire made good livings, those in the forest were obliged to subsist on a hunter-gatherer economy. The wildness of the country made it a haven for squatters with no fixed abode who lived in huts and survived as best they could on the fruits of the forest ... and a bit of poaching and smuggling. I well remember a visit to the forest as a schoolboy and finding in the heart of a wood a very rude dwelling and a man alongside. I didn't stay long enough to find out what he was doing, but he was probably one of the last charcoal burners, who built slow-burning stacks of timber and turf to make the sort of fuel now used on barbecues. This was the occupation of the legendary 'Brusher' Mills in the late 19th century, until he turned his hand to snake catching and captured the imaginations of the growing band of Victorian tourists.

THE BEAULIEU RIVER

The spirit of the New Forest comes from its heaths and woodland, but its few towns and villages are also worth a visit. The capital is Lyndhurst, where the verderers' court is held; it also has a visitor centre, which provides an excellent starting point for exploring the whole forest. Beaulieu and its river are major attractions, whilst Brockenhurst is a charming place, with the only rail station in the heart of the forest. Around the edges are Lymington, steeped in the sea, and Ringwood, a pleasant market town.

Until recent times, the forest was as easily reached by sea as by land. Lymington and Beaulieu

were the main ports and were significant commercial and industrial centres until the coal-and-iron logic of the Industrial Revolution put Hampshire in the shade. The first 'entrepreneurs' were the monks of Beaulieu Abbey. The scale of their farming endeavours is clear from the enormous bulk of the tithe barn at St Leonards, south of

Bucklers Hard, and the former fish-pond at Sowley to the west. After the dissolution, the Montagu family were granted the estate and to this day run it like the fiefdom it is. The limits of the estate are still marked by the heraldic signs of three red diamonds surmounted by a crown. The Palace House at Beaulieu, the Motor Museum and the entire village of Bucklers Hard are run as attractions for visitors to turn a noble penny or two. In the past, you might have seen iron being smelted at Sowley, the old pond used to power hammer mills, or watched the building of naval vessels on the Beaulieu River. Bucklers Hard would have thronged with shipwrights. Today, having passed the millennium lighthouse at the entrance to the river, and the Little Tern colony at Needs Oar Point, the waterborne visitor sees one of the best preserved waterways in the south, a benefit of privilege and power.

LYMINGTON – TOWN AND RIVER

Despite its easy access by road, rail and sea, Lymington still has the remoteness of that tiny market town that adventurous gentlemen and their ladies in their elegant coaches visited 200 years ago to breathe some sea air, visit the bath house and generally tone up. The artist Rowlandson came to record the scenes in his famous cartoon style and put the town on the map. It is still a fine jumping-off point for Yarmouth and the Isle of Wight; it was when making the trip to his home at Freshwater that Tennyson is said to have composed that famous poem *Crossing the Bar*. Today, as ever, Lymington is a place of the sea, with a jungle of buoys, masts and rigging, navigated by the shallow-draft ferry. It is one of those places which has made Hampshire the mecca of sailing: slip out of the Lymington River and go west past Hurst Castle and you are soon at the Needles, go east and it is Cowes and Southampton Water. No wonder that the Royal Lymington Yacht Club is one of the best in the country and that the yards, yacht designers, naval architects, sailmakers, chandlers and shipwrights hereabouts can build or fix just about anything that goes on water.

A pioneer of the yacht business was Thomas Inman from Hastings, Kent, who, in 1819, set up his yard on the river. His vessels were sailed by members of the Royal Yacht Squadron, Cowes, who found them to be virtually unbeatable. The tradition is continued today, with Olympics selectors always keeping an eye on

this corner of the county. Inman's business was later continued by an eccentric cleric of Romsey Abbey, the Rev E.L. Berthon, who invented various nautical devices, including the screw propellor (his claim!) and the collapsible boat, a sort of wood-and-canvas lifeboat that could be easily stowed.

Heart of the Forest

According to tradition, when William the Conqueror set eyes on this remote corner of Hampshire he decided that it would be ideal for *la chasse* and laid waste 36 villages and their churches. Modern historians take issue with the story, which is probably not literally true but reflects the opposition of local people to Norman forest law, which limited their rights in a way akin to the game laws of more recent times. The forest still has its own local laws, such that owners of certain properties have rights to grazing for a number of horses and cattle. In fact, effective management of the forest depends on these animals; in recent times ownership of properties by 'townies' has made it more difficult to rely on these traditional methods.

From Tudor times, the forest became an essential source for the oaks required to build naval ships. Hereafter, it was progressively managed in a much more directed fashion, with enclosures specified for particular crops and fenced to keep out deer and other animals that prevent small trees from becoming established.

After the death of William the Conqueror, his beloved forest featured in the nation's record in a way he could hardly have envisaged. His son, William Rufus, William II of England, a riotous ill-behaved sort of man, was killed by an arrow whilst hunting near the hamlet of Canterton, near Stoney Cross. The site is marked by the famous Rufus Stone. Whether it was an accident or an intentional assassination by Sir Walter Tyrrell who (perhaps wisely) fled the scene will probably never be known, though an accident seems more likely. The forest also claimed the lives of Richard,

another of William's sons, who was gored by a deer, and his grandson Henry, who was 'stricken by a bough into the jaws'. Such events no doubt endeared the place to Sir Arthur Conan Doyle, creator of Sherlock Holmes and other stories, who is buried in the cemetery of Minstead church (*opposite*).

BESIDE THE RIVER AVON

The limits of the New Forest, now designated a National Park, are clearly defined for administrative purposes. But even without a map it is easy to appreciate the change between the forest's relatively unfettered heaths and woodlands (though these are enclosed to some extent) and the more manicured smallholdings and farms that surround it. In Frimley with its charming pub and pond you are definitely in the forest (though a gunpowder factory once stood at this remote site). As you move north and west the countryside changes, under the influence of the rich meadows of the river Avon. More money was always to be made here, where grazing for cattle was lush and reliable waters turned mills, than on the acid barren lands of the forest. Ibsley, South Gorley, North Gorley, Hungerford, Frogham, Blisford – these are the villages where the settled ways of farming built long-lasting small communities, perhaps shunned by those who preferred to chase after wild animals and enjoy the relative freedom of the forest.

Fordingbridge (*inset*) is one of those places whose name, wonderful as it is, could have been agreed by a committee. The ford probably crossed the river near the church and the wonderful seven-arch medieval bridge still stands a short distance to the east. Its fortunes have been sandwiched between those of Ringwood downstream and its great neighbour of Salisbury to the north. The waters of the river once allowed it to support a considerable number of craft industries, including the inevitable brewery, together with flax spinning and the weaving of sacking, sailcloth and other kinds of canvas. Until his death in 1961, the controversial artist Augustus John lived to the north, at Upper Burgate.

SOUTHAMPTON – GATEWAY TO ENGLAND

The heyday of Southampton was perhaps when the rich and the famous came here from New York by luxury liner. The publicity machine made sure that every wave of the hand, every new fur stole, and every diamond necklace got full exposure. It gave the town (only a city since 1964) a glamour which was, however, hugely misplaced, as most of its inhabitants knew. For the main business of Southampton lies in the more pedestrian tasks of building, repairing, docking, stocking and generally attending to the many needs of sea-going vessels. It now boasts that it is the 'home of ocean sailing'. And each year in the autumn the International Southampton Boat Show brings yachties and non-yachties alike from far and wide. Some of the sparkle of the past has also been regained by the cruise business, especially since *Queen Mary 2* appeared in Southampton's waters (though almost all of her time is spent at sea).

The early days of Southampton as a modern port were prompted by the arrival of the railway from London in 1840. It was only twenty years since the first steamship, the *Prince of Coburg*, had gone into service between Southampton and Cowes and capital for an ambitious scheme of docks and basins was difficult to obtain. Yet when the Outer Dock (now called Princess Alexandria dock) was opened in 1842 it was enthusiastically used by P & O for carrying the mails to India, Spain and Portugal ('the peninsula'), and the Mediterranean in general. The government also turned its back on Falmouth and decided to make Southampton its principal Packet Station. Things were looking up for a town which had fallen on hard times after the middle ages and had become a 'watering place' frequented by the polite company of the likes of novelist Jane Austen and her family. Providing ship owners with the facilities they needed is, however, a hard business. In 1881 P & O moved to London and it was 80 years before they could be lured back. Yet for all its success as a dock town, Southampton is likely to be remembered as the place from which the *Titanic* set sail in 1912. The story refuses to stop running! Many local people lost their lives and their suffering is reflected in several memorials around the city.

EARLY SOUTHAMPTON

•

The huge sprawl of modern Southampton obscures the kernel of the place, which lies between Above Bar and Town Quay and is easily explored on foot. So much of the ancient medieval walls survive that the outlines of the old town can be followed in a wall walk. Particularly interesting for the visitor are the buildings that lined the old waterfront and the basins of the early Victorian eastern docks. The modern development of Ocean Village is centred around the Royal Southampton Yacht Club and the mall Canute's Pavilion (it was at Southampton that King Canute, who was obviously well briefed on the local double tides, 'stopped the sea'). The story of the town is told in the Maritime Heritage Centre, but to taste its 'salt' needs a cruise in the *Shield Hall*, the last sea-going steamer in the world or a shore-side view of one of the ocean yacht races that from time to time start here. Nearby is the Southampton Hall of Aviation, which tells, amongst other things, the thrilling story of R.J Mitchell and the Spitfire, designed and built hereabouts.

The city's Museum of Archaeology is housed in a former defence works, God's House Tower. This shows Southampton to have been a major port in the middle ages, especially for wool, wine and a variety of Mediterranean imports. It also tells the story of two previous port centres further upstream, namely, Hamwic the Saxon port in the St Mary's district and Clausentum the Roman port at Bitterne. Hence the derivation of the city's name: 'south of Hamwic town'. The medieval wool trade flourished because English farmers with English weather had good grazing for sheep and continental tradesmen had the skills to weave cloth. The Wool House, a solid stone building used by the monks of Beaulieu Abbey, and now the Maritime Heritage Centre, still stands as a sign of the extent of the trade. Nearby is a memorial to the Pilgrim Fathers, who left Southampton for the New World in 1620.

For modern visitors, 'West Quay' is a shopping centre, but the West Quay proper was once the town's main port area, now marooned by land reclamation. It and its associated buildings such as the Merchant's House (*opposite*) bring alive the old quay, from which Henry V and his troops famously left for Agincourt.

The Tudor House (*inset*) is a venerable 500-year-old building on Bugle Street which, today, houses a museum. The gardens include the renowned knot garden.

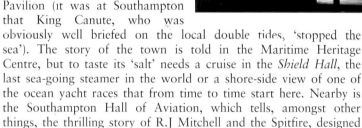

SOUTHAMPTON – CITY ON THE MOVE

The city is fortunate that its future is not based on a single factor. It seems sure to keep it status as a high-profile liner and container port, though recent attempts to expand on the opposite shore of Southampton Water, which is close to the New Forest, have failed

planning consent. As a ferry port it continues to vie with its neighbours Portsmouth and Poole. And as a cultural and commercial centre in its own right it goes from strength to strength. The docks are still a vital part of the local economy, but the city's traditional maritime industrial base has widened to include a huge range of manufacturing and service businesses. It is also a major cultural centre in central southern England, with a university, the studios of BBC South and Meridian TV, and extensive sports facilities, including the new Friends Provident St Marys stadium for football and the fabulous Hampshire Rosebowl for cricket. Shopping, too, has been transformed in recent years, with the focus shifted to West Quay from Above Bar, the traditional shopping hub which takes its name from the impressive northern gateway in the medieval walls (*inset*).

Much of Southampton's success is due to the fact that the city is sought after as a place to live in. The city's publicity people scarcely have to lift a pen to show that it has the attributes of a modern city and yet is within a sea breeze of the Isle of Wight, and a pony trot of the New Forest – as well as close to many attractive small towns and the historic cities of Winchester and Salisbury. It is a paradise for anyone who wants to raise a sail (or a kite), burn a bit of diesel on the water or, as seen here on Southampton Common (*opposite*), lift up and away in a balloon. For countrylovers there are few centres with as much to offer. Southampton is, in short, a city driven by its geography!

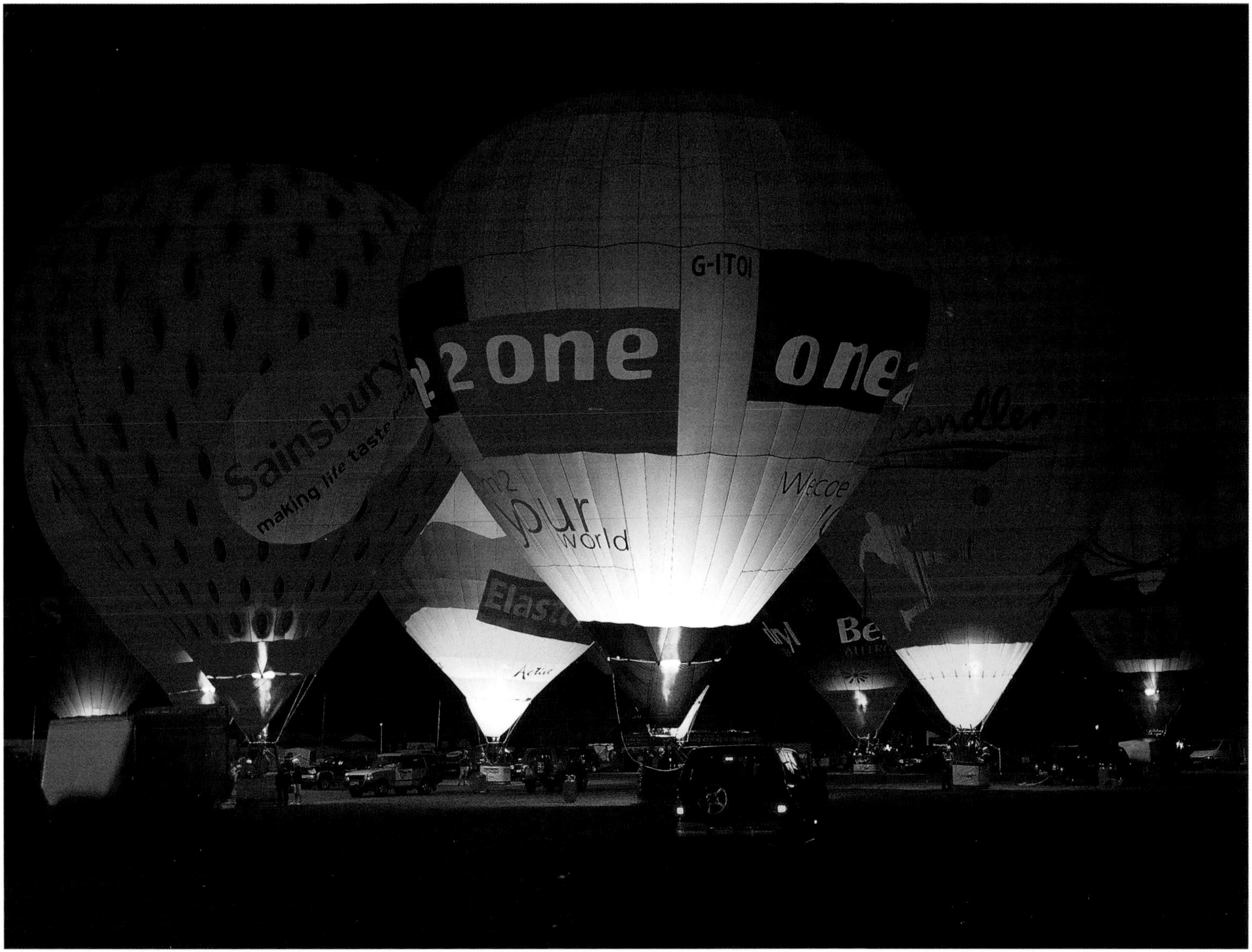

Sainsbury
making life taste
one
G-ITOI
world

ROMSEY – ABBEY AND TOWN

The constant waters of the river Test nourish Romsey (pronounced Rumsey by locals) and are the principal reason for its existence. The heart of the town and its ancient abbey sit on two islands in the river, which provided the defensive advantages that might, like the Île de la Cité and Nôtre Dame in Paris, have led to greater things if history had been different. The focus of the small town that grew up to serve the abbey is the square (actually a triangle), with its statue of Lord Palmerston (*inset*), the mid-Victorian prime minister who made Romsey his home.

The abbey church (*opposite*) was given to the town after the dissolution and is a wonderful relic of the community of Benedictine nuns founded in the early 10th century by the Saxon king, Edward the Elder, with his daughter Aelflaeda as abbess. She was followed by a succession of royal ladies 'so distinguished for their piety that they were regarded as saints'. Parts of the monastic buildings still survive under later façades and a rare Saxon rood can be seen. The church contains a remarkable 17th century memorial to John St Barbe and his family and an effigy of Sir William Petty (1623-87), scientist and man of business, one of the founding members of the Royal Society, who achieved great wealth from humble beginnings as the son of a Romsey clothier. For vigorous young male royals one of the virtues of Romsey was that it was a convenient place to stay for forays into the New Forest. One of the sights of the town is King John's House, a medieval hunting lodge discovered in 1927. Surviving plaster shows crude graffiti of the coats of arms of some of the knights who accompanied Edward I when he stayed here in 1306.

Until relatively recently Romsey was fêted as the site of Strong's Brewery, whose characteristic advertising hoardings were almost synonymous with Hampshire. It was the brainchild of publisher and banker David Faber, who in the 1880s bought up three small breweries and gave them a 'brand image'.

BREAMORE

The village of Breamore (pronounced 'Bremmer') lies to the north of Fordingbridge, just outside the limits of the New Forest on the western edge of the flood plain of the river Avon. It is one of those beautifully located places which suggests all the virtues of English country life and yet also has the knack of being interesting.

Today, most people who come to the village come to visit Breamore House (*opposite*), home since the late 17th century of the Hulse family, whose fortunes prospered when one of them became physician to George II and received a baronetcy. Alongside is a countryside museum with an extraordinary array of bygones set in realistic interiors. The lives of those craftsman that were once to be found in every place – wheelwright, blacksmith, bootmaker – are lovingly detailed. There is also a collection of carriages, those prized vehicles that gave every bit as much freedom to their well-to-do owners as the modern motor car does today. And, no doubt, they were regularly washed and polished and valeted – by the valet, of course – and the footman, who probably also spent spare moments buffing up the polish. But the prize exhibit is the Red Rover, the last of the stagecoaches to run between Southampton and London until the railway offered something better.

The existing Breamore House is a fine Elizabethan E-shaped house, rebuilt after a devastating fire of 1856. The original house was built in 1583 when the owner, William Dodington, took over the site of an Augustinian priory and associated tithes. He committed suicide in London by jumping from a church. His descendants 'reflecting on the tragedies that had happened' decided to restore the tithes to local churches. Breamore itself has a fine 10th century Saxon church, with

an extremely rare Saxon inscription carved on the arch of the south transept. It translates as 'Here the covenant is explained to you.' This is a place where history just seems to accumulate. A dozen hatchments still hang up inside the church: these are coats of arms of former owners of Breamore House which were put there after their funerals and just stayed there!

MONASTERIES – RUINS AND FINE MANSIONS

The remains of abbeys, priories, nunneries and other monastic establishments are often attractive ruins in pleasant surroundings, usually with a lengthy history displayed on a notice board. They were, of course, the forerunners of many of the public-spirited institutions of modern times – hospitals, universities, residential homes for the elderly and infirm. They were often founded and endowed by royal command or owed their existence to religious orders from the Continent. The extent to which they dominated local life is clear from the example of Winchester, which contained St Swithun's Priory (with the cathedral as its church), Hyde Abbey, St Mary's Abbey or Nunnaminster, as well as friaries for Carmelites, Augustinians, Franciscans and Dominicans – as well as the hospitals of St Cross, St John, St Elizabeth and St Mary Magdalen! When Henry VIII took charge of the monasteries most of them had only a few residents, but they still owned huge estates. Their relics and evidence of the changes wrought at this time are to seen throughout the county.

Many monastic sites were granted for relatively small sums to men who had served the crown well. One of these was Thomas Wriothesley, Lord High Treasurer and Earl of Southampton, who obtained the site of Hyde Abbey, Winchester. He quickly tore down the abbey and its church, the final resting place of Alfred the Great, and turned the estate to rent and development. Elsewhere, more sensitive changes took place, such as at Mottisfont (*inset*), where the Augustinian priory was obtained by the Lord Chamberlain, William Lord Sandys, in exchange for the villages of Chelsea and Paddington. He grafted a new mansion onto the old buildings, though most of what remains is that of a small house built in the middle of the 18th century. Netley Abbey (*opposite*) was a Cistercian foundation of

Henry III and at the dissolution was acquired by Sir William Paulet, who became Marquis of Winchester. The church was modified and occupied for a while but was never completely demolished. Its ivied ruins, in delightful wooded surroundings beside Southampton Water, became a cherished subject for artists and writers. Altogether, the relics of the medieval monasteries of Hampshire still have much to tell about life of another time.

OLD WINCHESTER HILL AND DANEBURY

Valleys are rich, but hills are safe. This is the dictum which helps to explain the siting of many early Hampshire settlements, high above the valley floor with wide-ranging views of the surrounding countryside. Many hill sites contain obvious evidence of earlier occupation, but it was not until archaeologists discovered how to conduct careful excavations and interpret the evidence of

finds that the gossip of folklore could be turned into fact. Excavation of St Catherine's Hill, Winchester, by Christopher Hawkes was an early example of the method and enabled the Iron Age site of *venta belgarum*, the town of the British tribe Belgae, to be described in detail. Old Winchester Hill (*opposite*), despite its name and the fact that it is surmounted by an Iron Age hill fort and several Bronze Age burial mounds, is not an early site of the cathedral city. Rather, it is in the parish of Meonstoke, which was in the patronage of the Bishop of Winchester. Today it is managed as a nature reserve, with shadowy yew woods and butterfly-rich meadows containing orchids and other wild flowers.

High above the floor of the Test valley, near Stockbridge, stands Danebury Hill (*inset*), which is a good example of a defended Iron Age site. It is encircled by well-preserved prominent earthworks, with a great eastern gateway, and was the subject of a 20-year excavation by Oxford archaeologist Professor Barry Cunliffe at the end of the last century. He showed that rather than being just 'a place for refuge' Danebury was a full-blown town, with a population of about 200-350 and a rich local economy. There were so many storage pits for grain that at the end of each season's dig the ground was described as being 'like a slab of Gruyere cheese'. Danebury enjoyed a stable way of life for a long period from 600 BC until about 100 BC, when it abruptly ceased. The reasons are not clear, but similar fates overtook other hillforts in southern England at a similar time, probably due to changes triggered by growing Roman influence in what is now northern France.

ANDOVER AND THE UPPER TEST

An artist sketching an imaginary map might decide to place a sizeable town at a suitable distance from another town on a tributary in the upper valley of a chalk stream. Such is Andover, situated on the River Anton, which runs into the Test nearby, which in turn runs down to Romsey and Southampton Water. Andover is at heart a pleasant market town. Its focal point is a fine town hall of 1825, but much activity centres on the modern shopping centre to the north and the industrial sites around the town. It has a fine Museum of the Iron Age, which is based on the finds at Danebury Hill and other sites and, nearby, Middle Wallop airfield is home to a very different museum – the Museum of Army Flying (*inset*).

to the source of the Test. The area has an industrial heritage that, contrary to all expectations, has probably helped to preserve it. This is the business of making the crisp, tough paper required for banknotes, first undertaken by the Huguenot émigré Henri Portal at Bere Mill, near Whitchurch. The most important contract he ever obtained was that of 1724, to supply the Bank of England with paper. As good as printing money! The business became centred at Laverstoke mill and is today owned by paper giants De La Rue. The Portal family, seated at Laverstoke House, once dominated the area, which contains many examples of their old-style benevolence and care for the river and its landscape. Whitchurch itself has a rare survival of the art of silk weaving, another industry well suited to the clear sparkling waters of the Test.

The Test valley above Andover is a delightful part of the Hampshire countryside nestling amongst rolling agricultural downland. The photograph opposite, taken near Overton, is close

STOCKBRIDGE AND WHERWELL

•

One of the finest stretches of the Test Way, a long-distance footpath that runs between Emsworth and the Berkshire borders, is that beside the river Test between Stockbridge and Wherwell (pronounced 'Wer-rell') pictured opposite. This is a part of Hampshire's waterside that has been recognised and cherished for a very long time. In the past century or two, the major motivator has been the need of well-to-do fishermen to preserve the world-renowned brown trout in the river. Just before D-Day, General Eisenhower no doubt had many thoughts on his mind, but chose (like Drake before him) to revive himself with his favourite sport. For Eisenhower, this was a spot of fishing on the Test. Sport of another kind was also once on offer hereabouts, namely, horseracing, the main racecourse for which stood on the high lands of Danebury Down and Chattis Hill, where stables are still to be found.

The centre of all this is Stockbridge (*inset*), which is a one-street town that has always been an important crossing point. The causeway on which the present road stands may have been laid down by Romans, though the town-cum-village proper was built in 1200 by the lord of the manor, William de Briwere, as 'the street' of nearby Kings Somborne. Upstream at Wherwell, a priory for Benedictine nuns had been founded in 986. Little remains of the ancient building which stood alongside the present parish church, though local history records that the estate was held by the monastery. An estate of a different kind was acquired by John Spelan Lewis, founder of the John Lewis Partnership. He created famous water gardens at Longstock and in 1928 bought almost the entire village of Leckford, where some 'partners' now spend their holidays.

Overall, it is the river and its wildlife that are the treasures of this part of Hampshire, where waterfowl and dragon-flies flourish on the crystal-clear waters, and huge trout rise to mayflies on warm summer evenings beside reedy banks. Long before planning laws became necessary, the people hereabouts seemed to respect the environment, where the softness of thatch and the warmth of brick complement nature.

THE HAMPSHIRE DOWNLANDS

Hills are inspiring places. The air seems fresher, the views are finer and there's nothing quite like being above it all. The hills of Hampshire are all on chalk, with gently rounded summits, sculpted dry valleys and long imposing ridges. They form part of the North and South Downs – not the highest lands in the country but equally revered by their localities. Portsmouth would not be quite the same without Portsdown Hill, from where the whole harbour can be scanned in the warmth of the car (the Millennium Spinnaker Tower will achieve a similar effect more expensively). Wintonians, as people from Winchester are called, can scarcely claim the name unless they have tramped to the top of St Catherines Hill and walked around the mismaze. And tales of tackling Butser Hill (*inset*), Stoner Hill, or the zig-zag path above Selborne in all weathers are part of the folklore of those from Petersfield and the Hangers country of East Hampshire. The name of the village of Steep at the foot of Stoner could hardly be bettered!

Elsewhere in Hampshire are less dramatic hills and hillsides, which nonetheless are places of refuge and recreation, such as Corhampton Down in the Meon Valley, Farley Mount near Winchester, Bury Hill south of Andover and Watership Down, near Kingsclere, which entered the national consciousness with Richard Adams' famous book. Cheesefoot Head, near Winchester, where a rock festival is held each year, is an example of the natural amphitheatres and other seemingly crafted shapes that can, to imaginative souls, suggest that the downs are more than natural features.

The north of the county comes to an end abruptly at an escarpment overlooking the Thames Valley. Nearby is Walbury Hill, the highest point of the county (now just in Berkshire), 300 feet higher than Old Winchester Hill, and 50 feet higher than Sidown Hill, which lies in the park of Highclere Castle, alongside its smaller cousin Beacon Hill (*opposite*). These fine hills were once called the Hampshire Highlands and well deserve the title.

GRAND HOUSES – HIGHCLERE CASTLE AND THE VYNE

Hampshire has more than its fair share of stately homes, several owned by the National Trust. It has always been close enough to the sea and to London for the wealthy to find a suitable spot to build their pile. The dissolution of the monasteries gave rise to several grand houses, all of which are open to the public, including The Palace House Beaulieu, Mottisfont Abbey and Place House, Titchfield. The owner of Mottisfont Abbey was William Lord Sandys, who also owned The Vyne (*inset*) at Sherbone St John, a mansion that was later developed into the present splendid house by Chaloner Chute, Speaker of the House of Commons, and his descendants. A state benefit of another kind resulted in Stratfield Saye House, which was given to the Duke of Wellington 'by a grateful nation' after the triumph of Waterloo. Nearby West Green House was also owned by a soldier, General 'Hangman' Hawley, who helped to massacre the Scots at Culloden.

Most of the grand houses still standing in Hampshire are the result of someone's bold imagination and careful management by their heirs. These include, the Georgian mansion of Hinton Ampner House, near Alresford, and nearby Avington House, which was a convenient place for Charles II to dally with Nell Gwyn whilst his palace was being built at Winchester. Northington Grange, also near Alresford, is a fine 18th-century classical building that almost went beyond repair but has been restored in recent years to become a nationally renowned venue for performances of opera in the summer. Broadlands House, Romsey, and Southwick House, near Portsmouth, were also both in their different ways the centres of large, well-managed estates. They both also have strong links with the Second World War, Southwick House as the command centre for the D-Day landings and Broadlands as the home of Lord Mountbatten of Burma.

Perhaps the finest grand house in the county is Highclere Castle (*opposite*). At first sight it looks like the Houses of Parliament, which is not surprising as the two buildings had the same architect, Sir Charles Barry. It was built in 1840 for the 3rd Earl of Carnarvon

on a site that was once held a palace of the bishops of Winchester. His descendant the 5th Earl put the place on the map when he financed the exploration of the Valley of the Kings by Howard Carter in the 1920s. The house contains many of his finds.

THE ROMANS IN HAMPSHIRE

The topography of Hampshire is largely Saxon and its older buildings are mostly from the 16th and 17th centuries. The long strings of pretty riverside villages that are a distinctive feature of the county were almost all originally settled by the Anglo-Saxons who came after the collapse of the Roman Empire. The British or Celtic peoples who preceded them, many of whom adopted Roman ways, were no match for these Germanic and Scandinavians adventurers. Yet for 400 hundred years before the arrival of the Saxons the country south of Hadrian's Wall had, of course, been occupied and governed by Romans.

The most enduring feature of the Roman period in the county is Portchester Castle (see page 74), the best-preserved fort of its kind in Europe, which protected the site of a major port at the head of Portsmouth Harbour. The Romans also made great use of Clausentum, near present-day Bitterne, at the head of Southampton Water. Winchester was an important, walled urban centre, with a forum, and a main thoroughfare which is still followed by the High Street. The Romans improved the site of the town by engineering the River Itchen to improve drainage and supply fresh water. North of Basingstoke lies the site of Silchester (*opposite*), once a full-blown Romano-British town but now a rural site with just a few relics. Most of the finds are in Reading Museum, but there are two fine mosaics in the entrance hall of Stratfield Saye House, whose owners, the dukes of Wellington, owned the site of the town until it was sold to the county in 1972.

The remains of several Roman villas have been found in Hampshire, but the finest is at Rockbourne (*inset*), near Breamore. Said to be the largest of its kind in the country, it was discovered in 1942 by a ferreter and excavated by a local estate agent, A. T. Morley Hewitt. Now owned by the county, it and its museum are open to the public. Amongst the finds are many examples of New Forest Ware, made in large quantities in local potteries, which were studied in detail by architect turned archaeologist George Heywood Sumner, who lived at South Gorley, near Fordingbridge.

BASINGSTOKE – OLD TOWN, NEW TOWN

Hidden in the centre of the modern town of Basingstoke is an old market town that was an important borough connected to the Thames via the Basingstoke Canal and the river Wey. As well as a weekly market, it held an annual wool fair and regular fairs for cattle and other animals, and an annual 'hiring day for servants'. Amongst its claims to fame are the facts that Burberry coats were first made here, Alfred Milward the shoe retailer first set up in the town, and it is the birthplace of the founder of Merton College, Oxford. In the 1960s and 1970s, old Basingstoke was changed utterly by a development group set up under legislation to move London's overspill population to the shires. The resulting modern town, with a population five times larger, has become a major force in the economy of the county, with huge shopping centres, a theatre, museum and art gallery, ice rink, swimming pools, athletics track and other sports facilities. It is the home of many well-known companies and other institutions, including the Automobile Association, the Civil Service Commission, and Macmillans the publishers.

Like many towns, old Basingstoke struggled to improve its links with London, mainly to take corn to market and bring back coal. Its first attempt in 1769 was in a northerly direction via the river Loddon, which rises near Basingstoke and runs into the Thames east of Reading. Eventually in 1796 a more effective route was found via Fleet, Aldershot and Woking to join the Wey Navigation at West Byfleet. It required 37 locks and a tunnel 1,230 yards long at Greywell. Heroic efforts by narrow boat enthusiasts and local authorities have now restored the canal to working order, so that a project which never brought any significant returns for its investors can be enjoyed by all. The western end of the canal skirts the village of Old Basing and the ruins of Basing House, which fell to Cromwell in 1645 after a two-year siege.

VILLAGES GALORE

'Famous for fifteen minutes' is a phrase that could be applied to even the smallest places of Hampshire. Traditionally, noble patronage was very effective in giving life to remote communities: at Kings Somborne it was John of Gaunt; at East Stratton the dukes of Bedfords and the Barings; at Titchfield the earls of Southampton. Other places have been put in the map by a successful business, such

as Taskers and Abbots Ann, Portals and Laverstoke, or by a craftsman like Edward Barnsley at Froxfield, near Petersfield. And Hambledon has, of course, basked in the glory of its claim to be the birthplace of cricket. But a famous birth, death or burial will keep people coming for ever!

Large places tend to head the 'burial league', with Winchester claiming Jane Austen, William Rufus and Alfred the Great and a large number of Saxon kings. But the Crimean War heroine Florence Nightingale was buried at East Wellow and the creator of Sherlock Holmes Sir Arthur Conan Doyle at Minstead, whilst Thomas Lord the promoter of the eponymous cricket ground ended his days at West Meon, where the notorious spy Kim Philby also lies. Wickham has perhaps been nourished by the fact that William of Wickham, the famous churchman and founder of Winchester College, came from here, but there seems to be a certain lack of any public acknowledgement of the fact in the village.

Writers of works that become classics have a head start over mere mortals and it is doubtful whether any inhabitant of Chawton (*inset*) can live a day without reflecting that it was here that Jane Austen wrote most of her famous novels. The Rev Gilbert White of Selborne did the same for this small village in East Hampshire (*opposite*). His church, his house, the zig-zag path that he and his brother cut and, of course, his book *The Natural History of Selborne*, all evoke country life at a time when the Enlightenment was changing everything. Not bad for someone who stayed a curate all his life.

ALRESFORD – THE BISHOP'S TOWN

'Alls-fud' is roughly how residents pronounce the name of their town, meaning New Alresford, as opposed to the nearby village of Old Alresford, which was overtaken as the main settlement when the bishop of Winchester founded the present town in the early 13th century. It is a thriving place with a remarkable number of shops, pubs and restaurants for its size. Shopping is still a pleasure in New Alresford, which specialises in the unusual, including antiques, fine arts, crafts and dress shops. Virtually the whole town is confined to a simple T-shape, the main road passing along East Street and West Street, with Broad Street (*opposite*) at right angles, leading down towards the river. Nearby is the rail station, once a stop on 'the watercress line' that ran between Winchester and Alton and now operated by volunteers (*inset*). For many years it was a vital link for the local watercress industry, providing winter salad for city dwellers. A trip between Alresford and Alton (with connections to London Waterloo) is a journey in celebration of the age of steam, with comfortable seats and courteous staff to match. Tickets for the line's Santa Specials, and Watercress Belle and Countryman dinners are soon snapped up.

Alresford is at the head of the river Itchen, whose copious springs were cherished by Saxon kings. Subsequently, rights in the river from source to sea were granted to the bishop of Winchester, who engineered the area in a way that a local development corporation might do today. Alresford pond, which still stands beside a huge causeway-dam, was used to rear fish, power a mill and perhaps to provide a huge reservoir for sustaining water levels in the river. New Alresford is now a pleasant, unhurried, country town, but at one time it was as shiny as modern Basingstoke, and the head of development wore a cassock. Planners, had they then existed, would have had to approve a scheme that provided new facilities for a state-of the-art market in the aptly named Broad Street. Having spent so much time and money in harnessing the waters of the town, the bishop was keen to develop the town further and maximise his income.

THE ITCHEN AND THE TEST

In any place in the world you can meet someone who asks after the Test (*inset*) and Itchen (*opposite*). Invariably, it is the fishing that starts the conversation, but these two rivers also embrace a way of life and a landscape that is eternally English. And they also have made a strong mark on the county of Hampshire. The Test rises to the east of Overton and then runs via Whitchurch, Stockbridge and Romsey, to enter Southampton Water near Totton, where Redbridge marks the point of an ancient bridge and crossing point. The Itchen rises further east, near Cheriton, and runs via Alresford, Winchester and Eastleigh to reach the sea within two miles of the Test at the appropriately named former village of Itchen.

The geography of Hampshire has been strongly influenced by the ability to cross these two waterways, which are fed by never-ending springs from deep reservoirs of water contained within the chalk. They were immensely attractive to farmers, particularly Saxon settlers, who sought failsafe water for themselves and their livestock and probably moved up the rivers from the Solent. In the Middle Ages, when water power became as important as oil in our own era, estate owners and churchmen in particular recognised the significance of water, lots of it, and built their communities in places like Winchester, Romsey and Alresford.

Long-distance footpaths enable both Test and Itchen to be walked for most of their length. The landscape is a succession of small bankside villages, with the occasional large town, flanked by extensive water meadows where the 'early bite' of spring grass for cattle and sheep was an essential respite from the grip of winter. Crayfish were once a delicacy frequently taken from the rivers, but today it is fishing for trout (very strictly controlled) that draws most people to them, especially in the vicinity of Stockbridge and Winchester. The Houghton Club on the Test is intimately linked with the development of dry-fly fishing, whilst Abbots Barton on the Itchen gets its glory from the nymph, a type of sunken fly pioneered hereabouts.

THE SMALL CHALK STREAMS

The river Test is fed by a number of small streams that are less celebrated but equally attractive in their own right. The Dun enters at Mottisfont (where a fine spring fed the priory), running from its Wiltshire source east of Salisbury, via a string of villages. The Wallop stream meets the Test at Horsebridge and is named after the earls of Portsmouth, who owned much of the surrounding land. The Anton runs northwest from Andover to meet the river below Wherwell, the site of a Saxon nunnery, whilst above it the Dever joins from the east. From its source at East Stratton, this pretty stream runs through some of the most pleasant countryside in the county, via Micheldever (*inset*). Although it is much much smaller than towns on the Test and Itchen, Micheldever demonstrates the importance of water from the chalk. It is an unusually large village that first attracted the monks of Hyde Abbey, Winchester, and was then held by the earls of Southampton, the dukes of Bedford and the Barings.

The Bourne, which joins the Test at Hurstbourne Priors, is important in its lower reaches for watercress, but further upstream it is a winterbourne that dries in the summer and rises again in late winter. This delightful stream and its confluence with the Test are celebrated in the classic book, *Where the Bright Waters Meet* by H. Plunket Greene. Often overshadowed by the Test and Itchen, but by some reckoned to be prettier, is the river Meon, which runs under Park Hill, East Meon (*opposite*), via a succession of villages, such as West Meon, Corhampton, Meonstoke and Droxford, finally reaching the Solent at Hillhead, below Titchfield. The river is named after the Saxons who first settled here, the

Meonwara. It has no large towns, though Titchfield is a large village and was, at one time, one of the largest parishes in the county. The abbey (now Place House) held huge estates between the Hamble river and Gosport, extending inland to Curdridge and the bounds of Wickham. Until the river estuary became blocked by silt, the village could be reached from the sea via Titchfield Haven.

WINCHESTER 'HILLS' AND THE HOSPITAL OF ST CROSS

The local topography of Winchester has long been the single most important feature of the city. Situated in the lush water meadows of the river Itchen, within reach of the South Coast, and surrounded by chalk hills and productive terrain, successive occupiers appreciated the virtues of a place that could be defended and provided the essentials of life. 'Hills' is the nickname used by the boys of Winchester College for St Catherines Hill, the prominent down that rises above the city to the south-east. Until the middle of the 19th century, the boys were marched up the hill twice daily, 'whipped in' by prefects, and left to play. It was here in the Iron Age that the Belgae, a Celtic people who dominated southern England before the Roman conquest, had a large hilltop town (*venta belgarum*).

At the foot of the hill, on the other side of the Itchen, is the Hospital of St Cross (*opposite and inset*). It was founded in 1136 by Bishop Henry of Blois, during a period of bleak civil war and famine in England. The bishop, who was also the king's brother, conceived the idea of a shelter and secure home for the 'poor in Christ'.

The great chapel at the hospital exhibits a variety of architectural styles reflecting the long period over which it was built. It is, though, essentially late Norman and is St Cross's greatest glory.

The Wayfarer's Dole is a custom which refuses to die at the hospital. Ask for it at the porter's lodge and you will be given a piece of bread and a small glass of beer. It is a relic from the Middle Ages, when the roads thronged with poor men and pilgrims, and charitable institutions were set up by the church to serve them. Despite its ancient buildings, St Cross is still a 'working charity', for it is a retirement home for men.

Winchester – the Capital City

Like most former capital cities, Winchester does not forget its times of glory. It was in 662 AD that Cenwalh king of Wessex transferred his father's newly-founded bishopric from Dorchester-on-Thames to Winchester, which became the capital place of the West Saxon kings. Thereafter, the seven major Saxon kingships of England vied for power until the late 9th century, when Alfred the Great united them against a common enemy, the Vikings. Winchester itself had suffered in 860 AD, when a large army came up from the sea, laid waste to the city and carried off 'immense booty'. Alfred's generalship eventually brought peace and he became the dominant Saxon leader, with Winchester as his capital. It became the largest of the 33 *burhs* which he created throughout Southern England. These were well-defended, walled towns within which trades and crafts could be peacefully pursued. The first 'King of All England' was Alfred's grandson Edgar, who reigned in the second half of the 10th century.

The palace where Alfred lived lies a short distance to the west of the cathedral (*inset*). Since most of his subjects could not read Latin, he encouraged the production of works in the vernacular Anglo-Saxon, and seems to have actively engaged in the writing and editing of them. He produced a manual of English law, which was kept at Winchester, and also started the Anglo-Saxon Chronicle, a key source for historians that charts the Saxon colonisation over a period of 300 years. He was a great patron of the church, not only at home but also in Brittany and Ireland. In Winchester he founded, with his queen, the Nun's Minster, which is still recalled by names such as Abbey Gardens and Abbey Mill. He also laid plans for the New Minster, a great church alongside the original Old Minster, which is now partly overlain by the cathedral. His remains were initially laid to rest by his son in the new church, but more than 100 years later, when the New Minster was demolished, they were reburied in the Hyde area of the city, where the lines of the abbey church built in his honour have recently been uncovered. After his death, the city flourished as a centre of the arts and learning, notably the production of lavishly illustrated manuscripts in the Winchester Style, with much gold leaf and stylised acanthus leaves.

MEDIEVAL WINCHESTER

When William the Conqueror crossed the Channel in 1066 he knew that the largest city in the realm was London, but first he took Winchester. The Hampshire city was in the hands of Edward the Confessor's widow, Edith, who surrendered to the invaders and sent out local people with gifts. William was subsequently crowned at Westminster, on Christmas Day, but he was also crowned in Winchester two years later and 'wore the crown' in the Wessex capital each year at Easter. Thereafter, as elsewhere, the Normans transformed the city. Some of the work can still be seen, notably in the transepts of the cathedral and the remains of the bishop's palace at Wolvesey. A palace was built for the king close to the cathedral and a fortified site on the western heights in an area still called The Castle and now occupied by the law courts and county council.

The Domesday Book was compiled at Winchester, though it excluded the city itself, presumably because its possessions were already well documented. This great record revealed that twenty years after the Conquest a mere five per cent of the total landed wealth of England was still in the hands of Englishmen. In Hampshire alone, the Norman nobleman Hugh de Port, seated at Old Basing, near present-day Basingstoke, held 55 lordships and the king held 67.

Winchester continued to thrive through the Middle Ages as a royal centre, and the seat of the most powerful see in the land, with several grand palaces, including Southwark in South London, parts of which still stand. Huge numbers of pilgrims also came to the cathedral to visit the shrine of St Swithun. In the 13th century, within the castle site, Henry III built the Great Hall, which was used for several parliaments and is regarded as the finest medieval hall after Westminster. It contains the Round Table (*inset*), a medieval construction that evokes memories of the legendary British king Arthur and his knights. At the end of the 14th century, the city also acquired its famous school, Winchester College, founded by William of Wykeham as a feeder school for his other foundation, New College, Oxford.

WINCHESTER – THE CATHEDRAL CITY

The Tudor revolution that led to the dissolution of the monasteries and the reformation were disasters for Winchester. Not only did the city contain a vast number of monastic foundations but its citizens took unkindly to the new faith. This was, of course, the period when the entrenched power of the church finally fell to the crown, to the great benefit of courtiers and other 'men of affairs'. A century later, the Civil War and English Revolution, which embroiled Winchester as it did many other cities, was fought on another platform of faith, albeit faith in the divine rights of monarchy, versus parliamentary power. And yet Winchester, with the cathedral and its community at its heart, despite the best endeavours of the Roundheads to destroy it, emerged from these troubled times to enjoy a period of tranquillity. This resulted from another royal edict, when Charles II, restored to the throne, decided to build a palace at Winchester and make it his country seat. He died before it could be completed and Winchester fell back into being a mere cathedral city. The grand barracks that came to occupy the site have in recent years been redeveloped to provide sought-after apartments.

Winchester, today, is a thriving small city that benefits, as it always has, from being 'not far' from London, from the sea, and just about any place of importance in southern England. It has become a sought-after place to live, with property values to match. And the crown law courts and the county council ensure that it still has the feel of a central place. But although it has been spared from the industrial blight of the last 200 years, it is not the cultural and educational centre it might have been. To be sure, it has its fair share of musicians, artists, writers and media folk, but it has only just acquired its university (University College Winchester, a successor to King Alfred's College, originally a teacher training college) and lacks a vibrant performing arts scene. For too long it has perhaps been overshadowed by the cathedral and college, lacking the will to escape its history.

VICTORIA COUNTRY PARK, NETLEY;
BUTSER ANCIENT FARM

It has only been relatively recently that local authorities have created places in the countryside where people can go for a breath of fresh air and the chance to experience some aspect of local heritage. One example is the Royal Victoria Country Park at Netley on the eastern side of Southampton Water. The chance to preserve this fine area of parkland was created in 1966 by the demolition of one of the high points of Victorian achievement, namely a military hospital (though its plans were derided by Florence Nightingale). Queen Victoria laid the foundation stone in 1855, too late to help the sick and injured of the Crimean War, but ready for the unfortunates from all those other wars, especially the 1914-18 First World War. The only building to survive is the green-domed chapel, a prominent seamark in the Solent, and now used to house a permanent exhibition of the history of the site and its surroundings. The chapel tower serves as a viewing platform. The hospital itself was truly enormous, with corridors extending for a quarter of a mile – so long in fact that when it was commandeered for American troops in the Second World War, they are said to have gone about in jeeps.

Queen Elizabeth Country Park, near Petersfield, is probably one of the finest of its kind. Covering about a thousand acres, it includes much of the dramatic chalk downland of Butser Hill, as well as the woodlands of Queen Elizabeth Forest. Nearby is Butser Ancient Farm, an internationally renowned re-creation of an Iron Age village, pioneered by the archaeologist Peter Reynolds. A central feature is a thatched roundhouse based on a similar one excavated at Pimperne, near Blandford. At Butser, archaeologists have attempted to create the style of life as it would have been 2,500 years ago, when the downs were farmed using simple ploughs and grain was stored over the winter in great pits dug into the chalk. These farmlands were worked for such long periods that, in many parts of the county, the ancient field shapes can still be seen, especially when the sun is low.

EASTLEIGH AND AROUND

Towards the end of the 19th century, the London and Southwestern Railway Company moved its carriage works to a site near to Bishopstoke Junction, where the London-Southampton line branched east to Fareham and Portsmouth and west to Romsey and Salisbury. Thus was Eastleigh created; it has now become a large borough in which Bishopstoke itself is a quaint historical relic. Not far away a similar process has taken place at Hedge End, alongside the M27, where a field name has lent itself to a major retailing and industrial site. However, Eastleigh airfield, where prototype Spitfires were put through their paces in the 1930s, is (perhaps not unreasonably) called Southampton International Airport.

Despite its image problem, Eastleigh and its surroundings are fun to visit. It has shaken off its railway heritage (though railway buffs will find all they need in the museum) and now thrives on a much wider commercial base nourished by its excellent communications and links with Southampton, Portsmouth and elsewhere. The centre of the town, with its attractive bandstand of 1903 (*inset*), bustles with activity, whilst its position alongside the river Itchen has been exploited by creating a huge country park. Some of the former estate lands of nearby North Stoneham provide excellent sport facilities, including Fleming Park, named after the former illustrious owners.

Wider afield, the countryside to the north and east of Eastleigh is very pleasant and includes a new-generation zoo that frequently hits the headlines. This is Marwell Zoological Park (*opposite*), opened in 1972 and devoted to preserving endangered species of animals. It made it reputation with animals such as the scimitar-horned oryx and the oddly named Przewalski horse, which is already extinct in the wild. Nearby Marwell Hall is on the site of a Tudor manor house belonging to the Seymour family: tradition has it that Henry VIII was privately married here to Jane Seymour.

CRICKET, THE COUNTY GAME

A large number of games played internationally originated in England. Yet, the process of throwing a hard, leather-clad ball at three sticks in the ground, and defending them with a piece of wood, and abiding by a complex set of rules, still remains confined to England and her former colonies. This must mean something – perhaps that of all the games played, cricket is closest to the English spirit. If so, it must also say something about Hampshire, for no other part of the country can lay a greater claim to its origins. The details still incur controversy, but the games of the Old Hambledon Cricket Club that were held on Broadhalfpenny Down, near the village of Hambledon, in the second part of the 18th century undoubtedly did much to put the game on an organised footing, rather than the occasional summer contest between *ad hoc* teams that it had been before. For all cricket lovers a pint at the nearby Bat & Ball Inn, even without any game in progress, is enough to evoke the ghosts of leather on willow.

Each generation has its share of doom merchants who predict 'the end of cricket', yet the game continues to attract its audience and the county has active leagues of village teams. There can be no greater statement of faith in the game locally than the money spent on moving the Hampshire county ground in recent years from its long-held site in the centre of Southampton to a magnificent stadium, the Hampshire Rosebowl, located on the outskirts of the city.

It seems strange that so much should have come from a small village like Hambledon, but in the past it was a relatively important place, with a thriving community. Like Alresford, but on a smaller scale, the short wide high street of the village leads up to the church and looks purpose-built for stall traders. Indeed, until the early 19th century a market hall stood here.

HAYLING ISLAND AND EMSWORTH

The southern coast of Hampshire runs from Emsworth (*opposite*) in the east to Barton on Sea in the west. It is a complex, indented coastline resulting from gradual encroachment of the sea, so that former river valleys have become the inlets and harbours beloved of seamen. The most obvious sign of this is the great bulk of the Isle of Wight separated from the mainland by the Solent, which has prehistoric remains on the seabed. Rivers on the southern shore of the county are closely matched by rivers on the north side of the island; they were all once tributaries of the Solent River. Similarly, the Needles at the west end of the island are remnants of a great chalk ridge that arched across to similar chalk stacks at Old Harry, near Swanage.

Hayling Island has been connected to the mainland by a bridge. The plans were the brainchild of William Padwick, supported by the then lord of the manor, the Duke of Norfolk, and were followed by the development of a posh resort on the south coast of the island, including the Royal Hotel and Norfolk Crescent, which can still be seen. But dreams of grandeur came to little and the beach is still Hayling's main attraction.

Emsworth lies at the head of one of the two main arms of Chichester Harbour, most of which is in West Sussex. It is a salty place, as befits an old fishing port, and grew up between two huge estuarine ponds that were impounded to turn tide mills. Like many others, the mill owners grew wealthy by selling flour to the Admiralty at Portsmouth. The town also flourished on local shipyards, whose owners developed an important local oyster and scallop trade in the late 18th and early 19th centuries. The Solent Way, which runs the entire length of the Hampshire coast, ends (or starts!) at Emsworth.

Hayling Island divides the two great harbours of Chichester and Langstone, which are joined by a narrow channel at Langstone village. Despite several schemes for commercial docks, Langstone Harbour has never been much more than an anchorage for small vessels, with strong tides at its narrow entrance. Since 1824,

SOUTHSEA

It was the Victorians who pioneered the delights of a holiday by the sea. Before the age of the package tour, the idea spread like wildfire, especially on the shores of Hampshire (including Bournemouth and the Isle of Wight, which were then in the county). Many people enjoyed the experience so much that they wanted to own a house by the sea, like the Queen herself at Osborne. A popular choice was the Portsmouth suburb of Southsea, which in the first half of Victoria's reign was extensively developed by the architect Thomas Ellis Owen. His villas were bought by people for the summer or rented by naval officers. The area was bounded to the south by the common, where troops from the Eastney garrison paraded. Southsea provided all that middle-class holidaymakers required. There were bathing machines, baths and reading rooms, and Owen built St Jude's church at his own expense. There was even snipe shooting at the recently drained marshes at Eastney. Medical needs were met by people such as the young Arthur Conan Doyle who in 1882 set up as a GP in Southsea and there created Sherlock Holmes and Dr Watson. He lived at 1, Bush Villas, Elm Grove ... very Southsea!

Seaside resorts, however, fall in and out of fashion quickly – each generation seems to find its own favourites. Today, for most people, Southsea is place to visit for the day or the evening. The seafront (*opposite*) is still its main feature – ideal for a stroll, replete with interesting sights on land and at sea. It runs continuously from Southsea Castle, the fort built by Henry VII in 1544, to Eastney, home of the Royal Marines. The centrepiece is South Parade Pier,

built in 1908-9, together with the period pieces found in many resorts – the floral clock, the rock-strewn gardens, the canoe lake. The main attractions are the Sea-Life Centre, the Pyramids Leisure Centre, and the D-Day and maritime museums housed in the Tudor castle. Built in 1984 to commemorate the 40th anniversary of the Normandy landings, codenamed Operation Overlord, the D-Day museum houses a remarkable embroidery 272 ft long sewn by members of the Royal College of Needlework.

NAVAL PORTSMOUTH

English history has been dominated by naval power, which for several centuries was strongly dependent on the dockyard at Portsmouth. Only since the last war has the city escaped its purely naval heritage and been able to gain some semblance of civic identity. The sheer scale of naval commitment to the area is huge – every scrap of coastline and vast areas of the hinterland are marked by the demands of naval training and operations, as well as defence in times of war. Even now, when naval vessels are sent to war, as happened in 1982 for the Falklands, and most recently for Iraq, Portsmuthians crowd the round tower at the entrance to the harbour to wave their loved ones farewell. The picture on this page shows the *Sir Belvedere* and the *Bustler* leaving Portsmouth.

A regular navy with vessels and men ready to go to war is a relatively new idea. In previous times commercial vessels were commandeered and men press-ganged into service. Nothing could be more different than the modern navy, with high-tech hardware, and highly trained men and women to match. Only at the end of the 16th century were special facilities built at Portsmouth to tend to the needs of ocean-going vessels. The position of the first dry dock built at the time was to fix the focus of the dockyard which grew up. The best way to view the vast complex that still exists is to go along to one of the annual 'Navy Weeks', or take a pair of binoculars on deck on one of the cross-channel ferries that use the Albert Johnson dock. Many of the buildings date from the 18th century and have a grandeur that matched the navy of the day. The centrepiece is still Nelson's flagship HMS *Victory* (*opposite*), though the Tudor warship the *Mary Rose*, recovered from Spithead, is perhaps even

more interesting. Just outside the dockyard is HMS *Warrior*, a fine example of a steel clad hybrid vessel that could run under steam or under sail.

The whole of Portsmouth Harbour is a delight for boating buffs, with much to see almost everywhere. On the Gosport side the history of the men who served on submarines is exquisitely told at the museum on the site of HMS *Dolphin*.

OLD PORTSMOUTH

Portsmouth is a city confined entirely by its geography. It is a vigorous, essentially maritime community bursting at the seams on Portsea Island, with overspill spreading up the A3 corridor and across the harbour entrance to Gosport. It is a place with a character of its own, quite unlike its more refined neighbour, Southampton, and completely at odds with its rural hinterland. It is, of course, at heart a naval city, though the local economy is now more widely based than ever. But, like many such port towns, it has drawn its population from all

Portsmouth's first port, defended by a castle, was built by the Romans at the top of the harbour at the aptly named Portchester. In the early Middle Ages it moved to the Camber, a small inlet just to the east of the entrance in an area still called Old Portsmouth. Car ferries run from here to Wootton, on the Isle of Wight. The shore side, overlooking Spithead, evokes the era when this was the cutting edge of the town, with the Round and Square towers, God's House church, platforms for gun batteries and much else. Here it was in the

quarters. London Eastenders are likely to feel more at home here than elsewhere in the country, reflecting the close historical ties with the great Thames dockyards. The virtues of Portsmouth which made it such an important naval base are that it has deep sheltered waters that are not far from London and are in position to command the English Channel.

days of Nelson that naval officers stayed at inns in and around the High Street, before being rowed out and piped aboard their vessels at anchor. The medieval church became the cathedral in 1927, when Winchester finally allowed its upstart charge to have its own diocese. 'Spice Island', as the area is called locally, was the traditional haunt of sailors on the razz and still is a place to go for a night out.

THE HAMBLE RIVER

The Hamble is no great shakes as a river. Rising near Bishops Waltham it is a small stream that scarcely merits attention until it reaches Botley, where flat-bottomed merchants vessels called pinks once brought cargoes of corn to within reach of the mill. Inundation of the Hamble valley by rising sea levels several thousand years ago made it a deepwater inlet of great utility to seamen. In fact, when the Tudors made a systematic evaluation of the ports and harbours of Hampshire to choose a location for a naval dockyard, it was a close run between the Hamble and its much larger neighbour Portsmouth Harbour. It is well sheltered and centrally placed so that, at the right state of tide, Spithead and the Needles are easily reached. Many naval wooden vessels were built on the Hamble, particularly during the 18th century at yards at Bursledon and Warsash.

Today the Hamble river, which is owned by the county council, is crammed full of yachts of almost every conceivable kind. Many of them slip their lines on a Friday evening and return on a Sunday, jostling for position at the entrance and making their way to the many for-and-aft moorings and marinas upstream. Many of them never move, for the river has a substantial live-aboard population, whilst some owners treat their boats as weekend cottages. But for anyone with an interest in the sea, the Hamble has everything you could ever need. Whether it's a trip across to the island, round the island, across the Channel, to the Med or even round the world, there is probably no better place to leave from than this Hampshire river, which is known throughout the world as a mecca for yachtsmen.

Landlubbers too can enjoy the Hamble, either by exploring the small communities on its shores – Hamble village, Bursledon, Swanwick and Warsash – or by walking along the footpath that runs along the whole of the eastern bank between Swanwick and Warsash. It continues along the Solent Way, to Portsmouth Harbour and beyond. A small ferry with a long history plies between Hamble and Warsash.

DEFENDING HAMPSHIRE'S SHORES

Portchester castle (*opposite*), standing at the head of Portsmouth harbour, has somehow survived for more than 1,700 years, and is the finest remaining Roman fortress in northern Europe.

After the collapse of the Roman Empire the inlets and harbours of Hampshire provided an open door for seagoing Saxons and later Vikings to enter and cruise upstream in search of plunder. The Vikings in particular got a bad reputation for violent assaults on

places such as Romsey and Winchester and one of the great successes of Alfred the Great was his creation of a navy to protect the shores. In the Middle Ages and later it was the turn of the French to attack southern coasts. In early October 1338 a fleet of fifty French galleys rowed silently into Southampton Water and fetched up at the foot of Bugle Street whilst the town was at mass. They murdered communicants in St Michael's church, looted and set fire to the town and vandalised the port. A similar party attacked Portsmouth. Edward III, who claimed the French throne, instructed the burgesses of Southampton to construct a wall, parts of which can still be seen.

Hereafter, defence of the Solent and Spithead became a major concern for all ages, notably during the reign of Henry VIII. Approaches to Portsmouth were protected by the building of Southsea castle at a point where the deep-water channel runs close to the shore. Hurst Narrows were defended by a fort on the Hampshire shore (*inset*), now embedded in a later Victorian fort, whilst approaches to Southampton were put in the firing line of Calshot castle. These, and many other defences, like the two castles or 'Cowes' at the entrance to the river Medina, made it difficult for enemy navies to enter the Solent with impunity. Three centuries later, at a time when French intentions were still uncertain, and the range of cannon much greater, Prime Minister Palmerston ordered the building of sea forts in Spithead and a ring of land forts at strategic points around Portsmouth Harbour. Dubbed 'Palmerston's Follies' most of these forts still exist and some are open to the public, including Spit Bank Fort off the Gosport shore.

WIND AND WATER

Mills of all kinds were once to be found almost everywhere in Hampshire. Some of them are still operated occasionally, like the windmill at Bursledon (*opposite*), the tidemill at Eling and the city mill at Winchester, owned by the National Trust. Hampshire has always been a fruitful place to grow corn, and the great naval base at Portsmouth gave it a major market not available to other shires. The corn was stored in characterful brick-and-timber granaries, raised on staddlestones, which are a common sight in the county. Medieval estate tithe barns, too, like those to be seen at Titchfield, St Leonards and Old Basing, show that corn has always been plentiful in the county.

Hampshire is also fortunate to have constant waters in its chalk streams and a twice daily flood in its harbours. Hence, the Test, Itchen, Avon, Meon and other rivers are dotted with water mills, many of which are recorded in the Domesday Book. Mill Lane, Abbots Worthy, even appears as *mylan weges* in a Saxon land charter. Until the late Tudor period, many Hampshire towns had thriving cloth industries that used water power for at least some processes. Fulling, for example, which is the process whereby good quality woollen cloth is made by pounding loose-woven cloth with tiny wooden hammers, made use of water power (eg the Fulling Mill on the Itchen near Alresford). Silk is still woven at Whitchurch on the Test, albeit now powered by electricity.

The tidemill at Eling, at the head of Southampton Water, ceased

commercial use in 1939. It is turned by water impounded at high water in the valley of the Bartley Water, a small stream that rises near Lyndhurst. The two existing wheels are 11 feet 5 inches in diameter and were cast at Ringwood in the days when most towns had local foundries. Operating such a mill for 'open days' is one thing; operating it day in day out at all hours, according to the tides, is another.

CLOSE TO THE LAND

A hundred years ago the vast majority of people in the county – certainly outside the coastal areas – were in some way involved with agriculture. In particular, it was known for its hops, still grown around Alton and in other parts of East Hampshire. Water meadows were maintained beside the chalk streams to provide grazing for animals, especially in the late winter when supplies of hay were exhausted. Hampshire also had extensive orchards and cider making was widespread. Honey was an important product, especially 'Down Honey' which, as its name suggests, was characteristic of the flavours of flowers and herbs of the chalk hills.

The traditional Hampshire sheep, which for centuries supplied wool for trading with the continent, was horned and whitefaced. From about 1800 it was gradually replaced by the Southdown, which was renowned for fine wool, quick maturing and the ability to thrive on scanty pastures. Calling any resident of the county a 'Hampshire Hog' is not mere whimsy, for local breeds of pig were greatly prized, particularly the great beasts that thrived in the vicinity of woods and forests, growing fat on acorns and beech mast. Amongst the cattle kept by Hampshire farmers there was a preference for those bred in the Channel Islands, a half-French part of the world that has always had special links to Hampshire, physical (once by sea and now also by air), spiritual and administrative.

Certain types of farming in the county received a boost from the advent of the railways, which enabled produce to be transported quickly to London and the other big cities. This included strawberries, grown on the poor, but well-draining lands around the river Hamble, and watercress, notably around Alresford.

Hampshire has changed out of all recognition from the days when farming was its major industry. And yet, one of the most recent trends has been the return of the farmer's market. The one at Winchester is said to be the largest of its kind in the country. So, after all, the Hampshire Hog is perhaps still as close to the land as ever.